Pet Corner

HAPPY HERMIT CRABS

By Rose Carraway

Gareth Stevens
Publishing

Please visit our website, www.garethstevens.com. For a free color catalog of all our high-quality books, call toll free 1-800-542-2595 or fax 1-877-542-2596.

Library of Congress Cataloging-in-Publication Data

Carraway, Rose.
Happy hermit crabs / Rose Carraway.
    p. cm. — (Pet corner)
Includes index.
ISBN 978-1-4339-6295-0 (pbk.)
ISBN 978-1-4339-6296-7 (6-pack)
ISBN 978-1-4339-6293-6 (library binding)
1. Hermit crabs as pets—Juvenile literature. I. Title.
SF459.H47C366 2012
639'.67—dc23
                                        2011024746

First Edition

Published in 2012 by
Gareth Stevens Publishing
111 East 14th Street, Suite 349
New York, NY 10003

Copyright © 2012 Gareth Stevens Publishing

Editor: Katie Kawa
Designer: Andrea Davison-Bartolotta

Photo credits: Cover, pp. 1, 5, 13, 19, 23, 24 (shell) Shutterstock.com; p. 7 Jeffrey Hamilton/Lifesize/Thinkstock; pp. 9, 15, 17, 21, 24 (tank) iStockphoto.com; pp. 11, 24 (sand) iStockphoto/Thinkstock.

Printed in the United States of America

CPSIA compliance information: Batch #CW12GS: For further information contact Gareth Stevens, New York, New York at 1-800-542-2595.

Contents

A hermit crab has
a hard cover.
This is called its shell.

It keeps growing.
It finds a bigger shell.

It lives in a glass tank.

Sand goes in the tank.

A hermit crab has 10 legs.

It eats many things.
It likes apples.

Hermit crabs play
at night.

They like to dig.
This makes them
feel safe.

They do not like
to live alone.

They walk on people's hands!

Words to Know

sand

shell

tank

Index